I0616158

Echoed

Echoed

If I write loud enough,
will you hear me?

Mel Lord, RN

This journal belongs to

Unexpected death shook my world suddenly, teaching me the importance of cherishing every moment.

Losing a loved one to cancer showed me the slow, painful process of grieving while also finding hope amidst despair.

Both heartache and unanswered questions coexist after losing someone to suicide.

The murder of a family member exposed me to the rawness of trauma and the pursuit for justice .

Lastly, navigating divorce illuminated the themes of identity loss and rebuilding.

These experiences have not only deepened my empathy, but also provided me with a diverse perspective on grief. They have enabled me to connect with and support others on their own journeys through loss.

Creating a grief journal requires a profound understanding of loss and the infinite emotions that accompany it. My experiences with loss have uniquely equipped me to undertake this endeavor. Each of these experiences have taught me invaluable lessons about the depths of sorrow, the complexity of healing, and the resilience of the human spirit.

Thank you for allowing me the honor to guide you through your grief journey. It's going to be messy and raw, but it is also going to be healing and beautiful.

Giving your words a place to land can be a deeply therapeutic process. A safe space to express emotions and process the complexities of loss. In this journal you will be given writing prompts to expand on as you travel through your own grief journey.

Set aside a dedicated time to write each day, ensure this timeframe is free from distractions. Start each page by writing the date in the top right corner. Briefly reflect on your current emotional state or how you are feeling. Use the writing prompt to write freely without worrying about grammar or structure; the goal is to express your thoughts and feelings messily, openly and honestly. Capture the thoughts trapped in your mind. Turn them into words. Express them on the lines of the pages.

Remember, this journal is a personal tool for healing. Allow yourself the grace to write. Without judgment. Revisit entries as needed to reflect on your progress.

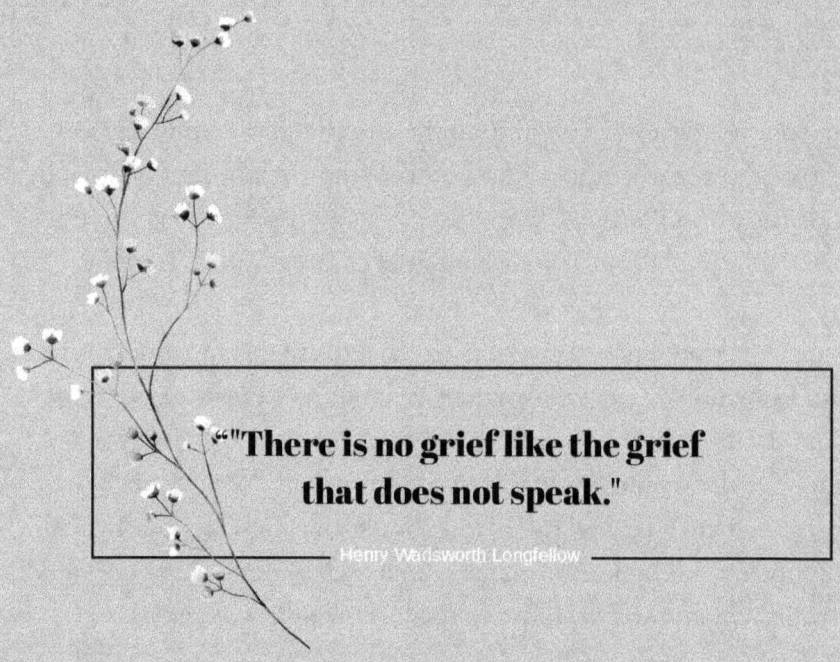

“"There is no grief like the grief
that does not speak."

— Henry Wadsworth Longfellow —

The Loss:

Briefly describe the event that led you here...

_____

_____

_____

_____

_____

_____

_____

_____

_____

_____

_____

_____

_____

_____

DENIAL
ANGER
BARGAINING
DEPRESSION
ACCEPTANCE

Initially introduced by Elisabeth Kübler-Ross, the stages of grief are a framework for understanding the emotional journey people often experience in response to significant loss. Note, not everyone will experience all stages, nor in a linear fashion. You can move fluidly forward and backwards through the stages.

My spin on the 5 stages of grief:

"Are you f-ing kidding me?"

Denial: This initial stage is characterized by shock and disbelief. It acts as a numbing barrier to the overwhelming reality of the loss. You might struggle to accept that it truly happened.

"I want to punch someone in the face!"

Anger: As denial fades, anger may surface. This emotion can be directed towards yourself, others, or even sometimes the person who has died or left. You might feel anger at the perceived injustice or circumstances surrounding the loss.

"If I ___ , will you ___ ?"

Bargaining: This stage involves trying to regain a sense of control by making deals with a "higher power" or dwelling on "what if" scenarios. It is common to ruminate over ways you could have prevented the loss or hope for a different outcome.

"Someone help me."

Depression: As reality sets in, sadness and despair may take a hold. This is natural and unfortunately, a necessary part of the grieving process. To retreat inside yourself is often essential to come to terms with the depth of the loss.

"I'm going to be okay."

Acceptance: This final stage does not signify happiness, but rather an acknowledgment of a new reality. Acceptance involves moving forward while holding onto memories and adapting to life without the person.

Reminder: not everyone moves through grief in the same fashion. You may move from one stage onto the next, then back two stages and then skip ahead three. Allow your process and stages to be as unique as you are.
Give yourself some grace.

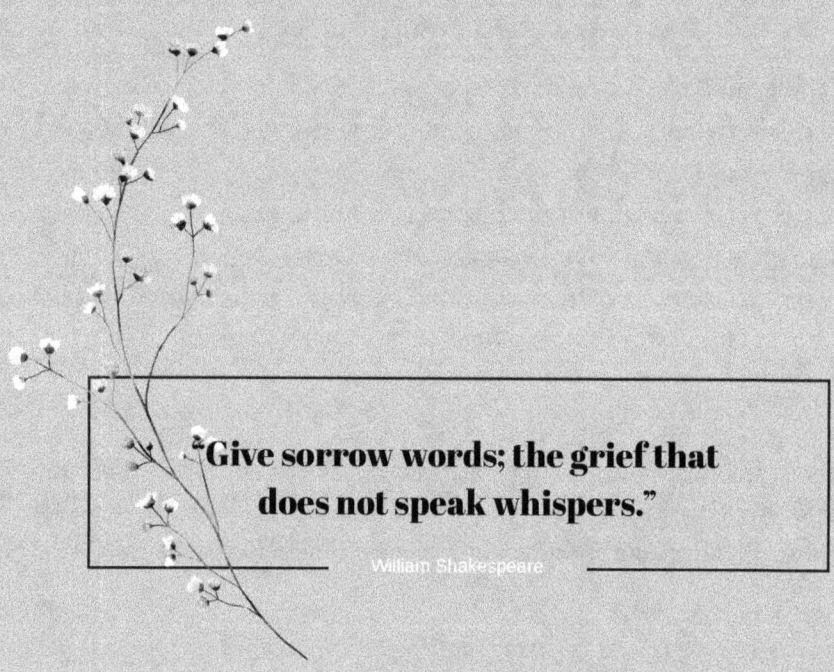

"Give sorrow words; the grief that
does not speak whispers."

William Shakespeare

Guidance for Journal Pages

1. Today's Date— Fill in the date you are completing the page. The date is helpful to remember as you look back on certain feelings and reflect.

2. Reflection— Take a moment to reflect on what has happened since your last journal entry.

3. Circle— which word most accurately represents where you are on your journey right now?

4. Set a Timer— 5-10 minutes is usually sufficient time to get your thoughts onto pages.
Don't feel like you have to stop when the time is up.

5. Journal Prompt— this is where you follow the prompt given with your own freewriting.
Don't worry about grammar, punctuation or spelling.
Turn your thoughts into words and get them onto the pages.

"Denial helps us to pace our feelings of grief. There is a grace in denial. It is nature's way of letting in only as much as we can handle."

— ELISABETH KÜBLER-ROSS —

ARE YOU F-ING KIDDING *me?*

DENIAL: THIS INITIAL STAGE IS CHARACTERIZED BY SHOCK AND DISBELIEF. IT ACTS AS A NUMBING BARRIER TO THE OVERWHELMING REALITY OF THE LOSS. YOU MIGHT STRUGGLE TO ACCEPT THAT IT TRULY HAPPENED.

Life has been completely shaken up, flipped upside down, and you are dropped back into your life and expected to go on just as you did before. There is no going back to how life was before the event. Life won't ever be the same. No matter how hard you try to resurrect the life you once had, once the loss has occured you are forced to move forward day by day, but life as you knew it will never be the same.

There is no linear guide map through grief. It is not a check the box on one stage and move to the next. It is more of a game of hopscotch. Shakily jump forward on one leg, then backwards again, leap forward with two feet, land solid….the next day your chalk outline of boxes has been washed away in the rain and you get to redraw the white dusty boxes and start all over again…one jump forward…

The beauty will return after the heartbreak. Your breath will lighten after despair.

Grief is messy. It is uncomfortable. Many times it is shoved down deep and completely ignored until it rears its ugly head a few months later in response to a song you thought you had deleted off of your playlist or the scent of jasmine on a warm May day.

… and so I write.

"

DENIAL
ANGER
BARGAINING
DEPRESSION
ACCEPTANCE

"

Set a timer for 5-10 minutes

Pick a word to describe how you feel at this exact moment in time.
How does it feel and why?

_____

_____

_____

_____

_____

_____

_____

_____

_____

_____

_____

reflect: 66

99

DENIAL
ANGER
BARGAINING
DEPRESSION
ACCEPTANCE

⏰ Set a timer for 5-10 minutes

The hardest part to comprehend is …

reflect:

" "

DENIAL
ANGER
BARGAINING
DEPRESSION
ACCEPTANCE

⏰ Set a timer for 5-10 minutes

What evidence do you have that this is reality?

reflect:

"

DENIAL
ANGER
BARGAINING
DEPRESSION
ACCEPTANCE

"

🕐 Set a timer for 5-10 minutes

How did you feel before grief?

reflect:

"

DENIAL
ANGER
BARGAINING
DEPRESSION
ACCEPTANCE

"

Set a timer for 5-10 minutes

What is your last memory before grief?

_____

_____

_____

_____

_____

_____

_____

_____

_____

_____

"

DENIAL
ANGER
BARGAINING
DEPRESSION
ACCEPTANCE

"

Set a timer for 5-10 minutes

My first thought in the morning when I wake is …

"

DENIAL
ANGER
BARGAINING
DEPRESSION
ACCEPTANCE

"

Set a timer for 5-10 minutes

Finish this sentence and elaborate,
"It is not fair …"

reflect:

> "
> _____
> _____
> _____
> _____
> "

DENIAL
ANGER
BARGAINING
DEPRESSION
ACCEPTANCE

Set a timer for 5-10 minutes

I can rely on _____ because ...

_____

_____

_____

_____

_____

_____

_____

_____

_____

_____

_____

reflect:

"

DENIAL
ANGER
BARGAINING
DEPRESSION
ACCEPTANCE

"

⏰ Set a timer for 5-10 minutes

Today, I choose …

reflect:

"

———————————

———————————

———————————

———————————

"

DENIAL
ANGER
BARGAINING
DEPRESSION
ACCEPTANCE

Set a timer for 5-10 minutes

I know I am avoiding …

"I sat with my anger long enough until she told me her real name was grief."

C. S. Lewis

I WANT TO PUNCH SOMEONE IN THE

Face

ANGER: AS DENIAL FADES, ANGER MAY
SURFACE. THIS EMOTION CAN BE
DIRECTED TOWARDS YOURSELF, OTHERS,
OR EVEN SOMETIMES THE PERSON WHO
HAS DIED OR LEFT. YOU MIGHT FEEL
ANGER AT THE PERCEIVED INJUSTICE OR
CIRCUMSTANCES SURROUNDING THE
LOSS.

Grieving; a verb no one wants as a part of their everyday vocabulary. To have grief, means that you have lost. Lost a person. A relationship. An idea. A job. Any loss can lead to grief.

"The act of grieving only comes as the cost of great love." Sounds cliche doesn't it? Having lived through great loss, unfortunately I can vouch for this bullsh*t saying. There is immeasurable truth in these words.

How do we "deal" with loss? When we are deep in the throes of sorrow, the last thing we want to do is acknowledge we have a scientifically studied, thus somewhat predictable process going on.
We have sadness.
Hurt.
Tears.
Heartache.
We have just lost and now we have to go through a "process"?

No thanks, I would rather sob into my pillow, scream at the dog and drink a glass or two of Sauvignon Blanc than think about going through stages of a "process".

… and so I write.

reflect:

"

DENIAL
ANGER
BARGAINING
DEPRESSION
ACCEPTANCE

"

⏰ Set a timer for 5-10 minutes

I have felt anger about …

reflect:

"

DENIAL
ANGER
BARGAINING
DEPRESSION
ACCEPTANCE

"

Set a timer for 5-10 minutes

I have projected my feelings by …

reflect:

"

DENIAL
ANGER
BARGAINING
DEPRESSION
ACCEPTANCE

"

⏰ Set a timer for 5-10 minutes

What is a constructive way that you can release the anger you are feeling?

reflect:

"

_____

_____

_____

_____

"

DENIAL
ANGER
BARGAINING
DEPRESSION
ACCEPTANCE

⏰ Set a timer for 5-10 minutes

Today, I will …

_____

_____

_____

_____

_____

_____

_____

_____

_____

_____

_____

reflect:

"

DENIAL
ANGER
BARGAINING
DEPRESSION
ACCEPTANCE

"

Set a timer for 5-10 minutes

_____ is someone I can confide in, without judgement,
because …

_____

_____

_____

_____

_____

_____

_____

_____

_____

_____

_____

_____

reflect:

_/_/_

"

_____

_____

_____

_____

"

DENIAL
ANGER
BARGAINING
DEPRESSION
ACCEPTANCE

Set a timer for 5-10 minutes

If I could take out my anger, in one way, it would be …

_____

_____

_____

_____

_____

_____

_____

_____

_____

_____

"

DENIAL
ANGER
BARGAINING
DEPRESSION
ACCEPTANCE

"

Set a timer for 5-10 minutes

I feel hurt when …

reflect:

"

_____

_____

_____

_____

"

DENIAL
ANGER
BARGAINING
DEPRESSION
ACCEPTANCE

Set a timer for 5-10 minutes

The physical sensations I feel when anger shows up are …

_____

_____

_____

_____

_____

_____

_____

_____

_____

_____

"

DENIAL
ANGER
BARGAINING
DEPRESSION
ACCEPTANCE

"

Set a timer for 5-10 minutes

It isn't fair, I want …

"

DENIAL
ANGER
BARGAINING
DEPRESSION
ACCEPTANCE

"

Set a timer for 5-10 minutes

If I could tell them one thing it would be …

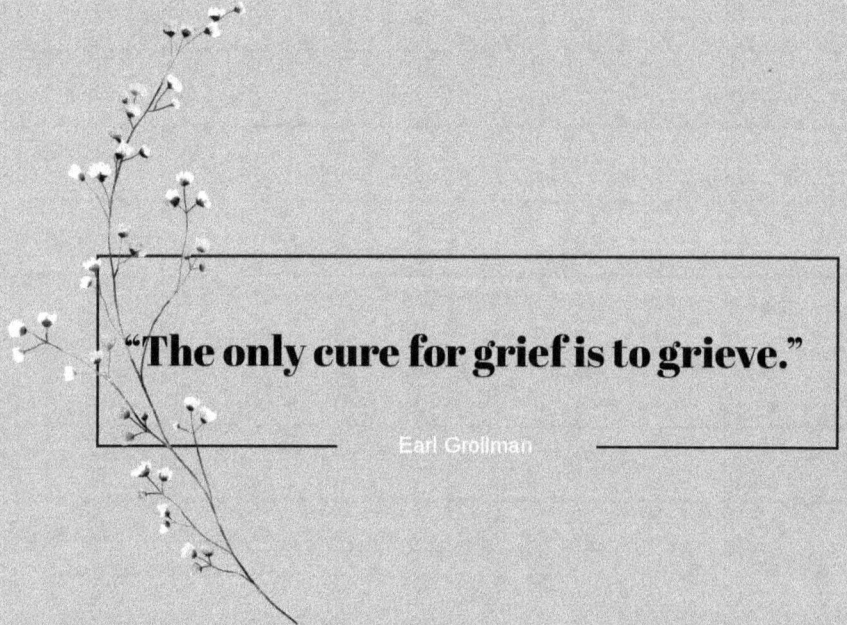

"The only cure for grief is to grieve."

Earl Grollman

IF I ___, WILL

you?

BARGAINING: THIS STAGE INVOLVES
TRYING TO REGAIN A SENSE OF CONTROL
BY MAKING DEALS WITH A "HIGHER
POWER" OR DWELLING ON "WHAT IF"
SCENARIOS. IT IS COMMON TO RUMINATE
OVER WAYS YOU COULD HAVE
PREVENTED THE LOSS OR HOPE FOR A
DIFFERENT OUTCOME.

"If only I had done …"
"I wish I would have said …"
"What if I had …"

I feel broken. Helpless. Ruminating and replaying moments in my mind. Trying desperately to rewrite the story that has already been written. Scene by scene. Line by line.

"If only I could …"

It's desperate, quiet, and lonely. Pleading with the past, with God, with the universe.
"This isn't right."
"Isn't fair."
"Fix it."
"Please, fix it."

… and so I write.

reflect:

" "

DENIAL
ANGER
BARGAINING
DEPRESSION
ACCEPTANCE

⏰ Set a timer for 5-10 minutes

I would give anything for...

reflect:

"

DENIAL
ANGER
BARGAINING
DEPRESSION
ACCEPTANCE

"

🕐 Set a timer for 5-10 minutes

What is one thing you wish you could redo?

reflect:

> "
> _____
> _____
> _____
> _____
> "

DENIAL
ANGER
BARGAINING
DEPRESSION
ACCEPTANCE

⏰ Set a timer for 5-10 minutes

I don't understand …

_____

_____

_____

_____

_____

_____

_____

_____

_____

_____

reflect:

"

DENIAL
ANGER
BARGAINING
DEPRESSION
ACCEPTANCE

"

Set a timer for 5-10 minutes

It hurts so much, I feel like ...

reflect:

"

DENIAL
ANGER
BARGAINING
DEPRESSION
ACCEPTANCE

"

⏰ Set a timer for 5-10 minutes

If I could trade places for one day ...

reflect:

"

DENIAL
ANGER
BARGAINING
DEPRESSION
ACCEPTANCE

"

Set a timer for 5-10 minutes

What is something to keep your mind busy today?

reflect:

"

_/_/_

DENIAL
ANGER
BARGAINING
DEPRESSION
ACCEPTANCE

"

Set a timer for 5-10 minutes

What do you feel daily?

reflect:

"

—————————————

—————————————

—————————————

—————————————

"

DENIAL
ANGER
BARGAINING
DEPRESSION
ACCEPTANCE

⏰ Set a timer for 5-10 minutes

I want to shout …

reflect:

"

_____

_____

_____

_____

"

DENIAL
ANGER
BARGAINING
DEPRESSION
ACCEPTANCE

⏰ Set a timer for 5-10 minutes

The secret I am holding is …

_____

_____

_____

_____

_____

_____

_____

_____

_____

_____

_____

reflect:

"

———
———
———
———

"

DENIAL
ANGER
BARGAINING
DEPRESSION
ACCEPTANCE

Set a timer for 5-10 minutes

Tomorrow, I will change …

"Grief is a nasty game of feeling the weakest you have ever felt and morphing into the strongest person you will have to become."

Windgate Lane

SOMEONE HELP

me

DEPRESSION: AS REALITY SETS IN,
SADNESS AND DESPAIR MAY TAKE A
HOLD. THIS IS NATURAL AND
UNFORTUNATELY, A NECESSARY PART OF
THE GRIEVING PROCESS. TO RETREAT
INSIDE YOURSELF IS OFTEN ESSENTIAL
TO COME TO TERMS WITH THE DEPTH OF
THE LOSS.

Eighteen months after the murder of my sixteen year old nephew, I sat with a close friend at a local restaurant. Condensation dripping down the sides of our short, salt rimmed glasses. She and I had shared a lot of life together over the previous 20 years. This was the first time I had seen her in the past eighteen months — by far the longest time we had ever gone without seeing each other. She apologized for not being there for me after losing him. She explained, "grief is just something I'm not good at."

I love her dearly. I understand.

Who wants to be good at grief?
I don't want to be good at grief.
Most days I suck at it.

My world had stopped spinning while everyone else's continued on.
I'm stuck.
Heavy.
Numb.
Smiles are foreign.
Conversations exhausting.

…. and so I write.

reflect:

"

DENIAL
ANGER
BARGAINING
DEPRESSION
ACCEPTANCE

"

⏰ Set a timer for 5-10 minutes

I feel _____ this week because ...

reflect:

"

DENIAL
ANGER
BARGAINING
DEPRESSION
ACCEPTANCE

"

Set a timer for 5-10 minutes

My last thoughts before I go to sleep are …

reflect:

"

DENIAL
ANGER
BARGAINING
DEPRESSION
ACCEPTANCE

"

🕐 Set a timer for 5-10 minutes

Today, I will do _____ for me because …

reflect:

"

DENIAL
ANGER
BARGAINING
DEPRESSION
ACCEPTANCE

"

⏰ Set a timer for 5-10 minutes

What does sadness feel like inside my body?

reflect:

"

Denial
Anger
Bargaining
Depression
Acceptance

⏰ Set a timer for 5-10 minutes

What side effects from grief have you noticed?

reflect:

"

DENIAL
ANGER
BARGAINING
DEPRESSION
ACCEPTANCE

"

Set a timer for 5-10 minutes

On a sadness scale of 1-10 today I am a _____ because …

reflect:

" "

DENIAL
ANGER
BARGAINING
DEPRESSION
ACCEPTANCE

⏰ Set a timer for 5-10 minutes

I choose _____ daily because …

reflect:

"

_____

_____

_____

_____

"

DENIAL
ANGER
BARGAINING
DEPRESSION
ACCEPTANCE

⏰ Set a timer for 5-10 minutes

My friends would describe me now as …

_____

_____

_____

_____

_____

_____

_____

_____

_____

_____

reflect:

"

DENIAL
ANGER
BARGAINING
DEPRESSION
ACCEPTANCE

"

Set a timer for 5-10 minutes

I make myself feel better by ...

reflect:

> "
> _____
> _____
> _____
> _____
> "

DENIAL
ANGER
BARGAINING
DEPRESSION
ACCEPTANCE

⏰ Set a timer for 5-10 minutes

A habit — I am not proud of — I have used to cope is …

_____

_____

_____

_____

_____

_____

_____

_____

_____

_____

_____

"Acceptance is not about liking a situation. It is about acknowledging all that has been lost and learning to live with that loss."

— ELISABETH KÜBLER-ROSS

I'M GOING TO BE

okay

ACCEPTANCE: THIS FINAL STAGE DOES
NOT SIGNIFY HAPPINESS, BUT RATHER
AN ACKNOWLEDGMENT OF A NEW
REALITY. ACCEPTANCE INVOLVES
MOVING FORWARD WHILE HOLDING ONTO
MEMORIES AND ADAPTING TO LIFE
WITHOUT THE PERSON.

The pain is less; not gone.
I am not over it, but it isn't consuming me.
I acknowledge this is my new reality.

The loss is permanent—I am still breathing.
My sun still rises and sets each day.
Grief has cracked me open.

I am restoring myself.
There hasn't been any significant breakthrough.
It has been a slow unfolding.

Life is different, but continues on.
I can carry memories, and not collapse under their weight.
I can laugh again.

I smile more than I cry.
I haven't let go of the loss,
just have learned how to harness it differently.

I have become more human in my heartbreak.

… and so I write.

reflect:

66

_____
_____
_____
_____

99

DENIAL
ANGER
BARGAINING
DEPRESSION
ACCEPTANCE

Set a timer for 5-10 minutes

Today, I smiled because…

_____

_____

_____

_____

_____

_____

_____

_____

_____

_____

_____

"

_____

_____

_____

_____

"

DENIAL
ANGER
BARGAINING
DEPRESSION
ACCEPTANCE

Set a timer for 5-10 minutes

I can see evidence that things will be okay when…

_____

_____

_____

_____

_____

_____

_____

_____

_____

_____

reflect:

"

—————————
—————————
—————————
—————————

"

⏰ Set a timer for 5-10 minutes

DENIAL
ANGER
BARGAINING
DEPRESSION
ACCEPTANCE

Tomorrow, I am looking forward to…

_____

_____

_____

_____

_____

_____

_____

_____

_____

_____

_____

_____

"

DENIAL
ANGER
BARGAINING
DEPRESSION
ACCEPTANCE

"

Set a timer for 5-10 minutes

A year from now, I will…

reflect:

> "
>
> _____
>
> _____
>
> _____
>
> _____
>
> "

DENIAL
ANGER
BARGAINING
DEPRESSION
ACCEPTANCE

Set a timer for 5-10 minutes

I look back and smile because…

_____

_____

_____

_____

_____

_____

_____

_____

_____

_____

reflect:

"

DENIAL
ANGER
BARGAINING
DEPRESSION
ACCEPTANCE

"

⏰ Set a timer for 5-10 minutes

I am grateful for _____ because…

reflect:

"

_____

_____

_____

_____

"

DENIAL
ANGER
BARGAINING
DEPRESSION
ACCEPTANCE

⏰ Set a timer for 5-10 minutes

What does happiness feel like?

_____

_____

_____

_____

_____

_____

_____

_____

_____

_____

reflect:

"

_____
_____
_____
_____

"

DENIAL
ANGER
BARGAINING
DEPRESSION
ACCEPTANCE

Set a timer for 5-10 minutes

I feel like I will be okay because…

_____

_____

_____

_____

_____

_____

_____

_____

_____

_____

"

DENIAL
ANGER
BARGAINING
DEPRESSION
ACCEPTANCE

"

⏰ Set a timer for 5-10 minutes

I am going to show myself I am okay by …

_____

_____

_____

_____

_____

_____

_____

_____

_____

_____

reflect:

"

DENIAL
ANGER
BARGAINING
DEPRESSION
ACCEPTANCE

"

Set a timer for 5-10 minutes

I will never forget, but I will…

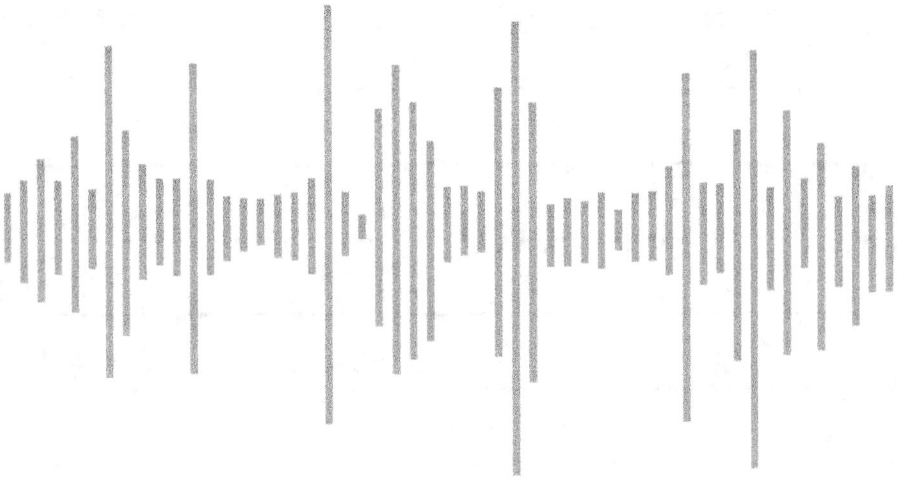

And so I write…
Loud enough for Me to hear Me.

I have graduated from the thinking that my writing is for others. It has
never been about others hearing me.
It is for Me.
By Me.

Every word that is translated from a thought onto blank pages, is another
step in healing. The words, locked behind emotions, that have not been
bravely formed. The words—when we are courageous enough to release
them—may be followed by a cascade of emotions. It is when we give life
to these words, a temporary cover is created on the gaping wound that
never seemed to heal. A wound that may appear to scab over at times. A
temporary barrier, between the outside world and the deep injury below
the surface. By identifying the words, and subsequently the emotions that
are to follow, we can begin to navigate a new way of life after loss.

We aren't immune to grief, just because we have lived it. We are not going
to be left without a scar after the scab heals. We can look at the sensitive
area of the scar, knowing our healing process helped to prevent infection.
It may be callused around the edges—sometimes a little raw—but it is
healed. Still visible. A new part of our being moving forward.

Thank you for healing with me. For allowing me to guide the birth of
your words, by delivering your once trapped feelings.

My hope is that You were able to write…
Loud enough for You to hear You.

Xo, Nel

MelLordRN.com

www.ingramcontent.com/pod-product-compliance
Lightning Source LLC
Chambersburg PA
CBHW071513120626
46550CB00006B/2211